GW00792840

FIRST FIE
COMMON
BIRDS
OF SOUTHERN AFRICA

Little Egret (page 16)

Cape Glossy Starling (page 49)

TRACEY HAWTHORNE

Contents

Southern African birds 4

How to use this book 6

Being a bird-watcher 8

African Penguin
Spheniscus demersus 10

Little Grebe
Tachybaptus ruficollis 11

Eastern White Pelican
Pelecanus onocrotalus 12

Cape Gannet
Morus capensis 13

Cape Cormorant
Phalacrocorax capensis 14

African Darter
Anhinga rufa 15

Little Egret
Egretta garzetta 16

Hamerkop
Scopus umbretta 17

African Sacred Ibis
Threskiornis aethiopicus 18

Greater Flamingo
Phoenicopterus roseus 19

Blue Crane
Anthropoides paradiseus 20

Red-knobbed Coot
Fulica cristata 21

Egyptian Goose
Alopochen aegyptiaca 22

African Fish Eagle
Haliaeetus vocifer 23

Black-shouldered Kite
Elanus caeruleus 24

White-backed Vulture
Gyps africanus 25

Ostrich
Struthio camelus 26

Common Moorhen
Gallinula chloropus 27

Helmeted Guineafowl
Numida meleagris 28

Blacksmith Lapwing (Plover)
Vanellus armatus 29

Crowned Lapwing (Plover)
Vanellus coronatus 30

Barn Owl (page 36)

Kelp Gull
Larus dominicanus   31

Speckled Pigeon
Columba guinea   32

Laughing Dove
Streptopelia senegalensis   33

Grey Go-away-bird (Lourie)
Corythaixoides concolor   34

Spotted Eagle-Owl
Bubo africanus   35

Barn Owl
Tyto alba   36

Pied Kingfisher
Ceryle rudis   37

African Hoopoe
Upupa africana   38

Crested Barbet
Trachyphonus vaillantii   39

Fork-tailed Drongo
Dicrurus adsimilis   40

Pied Crow
Corvus albus   41

Dark-capped Bulbul
Pycnonotus tricolor   42

Olive Thrush
Turdus olivaceus   43

Cape Robin-Chat
Cossypha caffra   44

Cape Wagtail
Motacilla capensis   45

Common Fiscal
Lanius collaris   46

Ostrich (page 26)

Fiscal Flycatcher
Sigelus silens   47

Red-winged Starling
Onychognathus morio   48

Cape Glossy Starling
Lamprotornis nitens   49

Amethyst Sunbird
Nectarinia amethystina   50

House Sparrow
Passer domesticus   51

Southern Red Bishop
Euplectes orix   52

Southern Masked Weaver
Ploceus velatus   53

Cape White-eye
Zosterops capensis   54

Cape Canary
Serinus canicollis   55

Glossary   56
Checklist   57

Southern African birds

Southern Africa is home to more than 900 different bird species. Not all of them are year-round residents, however – the 'jetsetters' of the bird world visit only for the summer or winter, flying north again when the season changes. Some Antarctic species visit southern Africa during the winter. Also, among our resident birds, quite a few are not easily seen – some are rare, and some prefer little-inhabited regions such as mountains and deserts, while others are nocturnal or very secretive.

Although only 46 species are covered in this book, many other southern African birds occur in large numbers in the region. Bear this in mind when you take this book with you on a bird-watching trip. The habitat map shown opposite will give you an idea of the different types of vegetation found in the region, while the regional map (opposite, bottom) shows the South African provinces, and should be used together with the distribution map shown alongside each species account.

Cape Gannets (page 13)

Habitats

Regions

5

How to use this book

African Penguin (page 10)

Each species account is split up into several headings, listed below.

Common name: The 'common name' is the English name by which the bird is known internationally. These have been updated in accordance with recommendations by an international committee.

Scientific name: This is the official name by which the bird is known throughout the world, and is always written in *italic* type.

Other names: The bird's name in Afrikaans (A), Xhosa (X) and Zulu (Z) – the most commonly spoken South African languages after English – where available.

Average size: The total **length** of the bird is given. This is measured from bill tip to tail tip, with the bird stretched out, so it will be slightly longer than the bird's measurement as seen in the field. Use the ruler on the outside back cover for a realistic idea of how big the bird is.

The **wingspan** (the measurement from wingtip to wingtip) is given where this information is available; otherwise, the measurement of a single **wing**, from 'elbow' to wingtip, is provided. Only where male and female measurements differ significantly are both given.

Identification: The colours of the bird's plumage and bare parts, as well as other physical characteristics that will help you to identify the bird.

Call: Difficult to put into words, this is intended only as a rough guide to the sound the bird makes.

Habitat: What environment the bird prefers. This, together with the distribution map that accompanies the species account, will tell you where a specific bird is likely to be seen. The southern African region includes South Africa, Lesotho, Swaziland, Namibia, Botswana, Zimbabwe and Mozambique.

Habits: The bird's social behaviour (for instance, whether it is gregarious^G or solitary^G) and its feeding habits.

Nesting: The time of year a bird breeds, the type of nest it builds, the number and appearance of the eggs it lays, and the incubation^G period of its eggs.
   Where relevant, the bird's breeding behaviour is also described.

Notes: Anything of special significance or interest.

Status: Most of the birds in this book are common residents, which means that they occur throughout the year in the region.

Food: What food the bird prefers.

Similar species: Bear in mind that in many cases similar-looking species do not necessarily occur in the same location or habitat as the birds discussed in this book.

A small, uppercase ^G after a word indicates that it is explained in the **Glossary** on page 56.

Egyptian Goose (page 22)

7

Being a bird-watcher

Some people become a little intimidated when setting out to watch birds for the first time – after all, there are so many of them, and they all look so similar!

With a little practice, though, you will soon be able to identify one or two species, and soon this number will grow to 10 or 12, and before you know it you will be a fully fledged 'twitcher' (this is the name given to fanatical bird-watchers who try to identify as many different species as possible).

What bird is it?

The first step in identifying a bird, aside from obvious things like its size, colour and where you have spotted it, is its 'jizz', which means its overall look and behaviour. If, for instance, it hops about energetically on the ground, it could be a sparrow; but if it is walking along slowly like a stately old man, it might be an ibis.

Bear in mind when reading this book that a 'small' vulture will obviously be much bigger than a 'small' dove. The length of the bird (given in

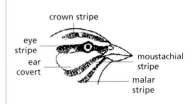

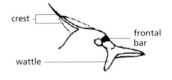

centimetres) and the ruler on the outside back cover will help you to compare the size of the bird you have spotted in the field with the species featured in this book.

Check these things to identify a bird

↓ What **size** is the bird you see?

↓ Study the **shape** of the bird, paying particular attention to its body, head, bill and tail shapes.

↓ Male birds are particularly colourful. Try to identify the **colours** of different body, plumage and bare parts (the parts of the bird are shown left and right).

↓ What is the bird doing, and is its **behaviour** normal?

↓ Where is the bird **feeding** or **nesting**?

↓ The distribution map will show you if the species you have spotted is found in your **region**.

Bird names

All birds have a local common name (for example, Grey Lourie), a scientific name (*Corythaixoides concolor*), and, sometimes, one or more alternative names (for example, Go-away-bird).

BE AWARE!
Don't disturb birds, particularly if they are breeding. Never touch their nests, eggs or chicks – the parents might desert their young if you have interfered with them. Watch from a distance, through binoculars if you have them.

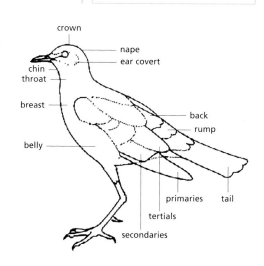

crown
nape
ear covert
chin
throat
breast
back
rump
belly
primaries
tail
tertials
secondaries

African Penguin

Spheniscus demersus

Other names: Brilpikkewyn (A); inguza & unombombiya (X).

Average size: Length 60cm; length of flipper 16,5cm.

Identification: A flightless bird whose wings are mere 'flippers'. Black chin and face patch, separated from crown by broad white band; narrow black band across chest and down flanks. Pink skin above eye.

Call: Loud, donkey-like braying at night; also honks and growls.

Habitat: Offshore islands and at sea; less often on mainland.

Habits: Lives in small groups on the coast or in huge groups on offshore islands. Forages underwater at sea, coming to land to roost^G and breed.

Nesting: Year round, mainly in summer. Breeds colonially^G on offshore islands. One or two white eggs are laid in a hollow dug into guano^G or sandy ground. These take five to six weeks to hatch.

Notes: Collection and selling of eggs, guano^G scraping, overfishing and oil spills have contributed to the decrease in its numbers.

Status: Resident endemic^G. 'Vulnerable'.

Food: Fish, squid.

Similar species: None.

Little Grebe

Tachybaptus ruficollis

Other names: Kleindobbertjie (A); unolwilwilwi & unoyamembi (X).

Average size: Length 20cm; wing 9–10cm.

Identification: Blackish above, pale rufous^G below. Creamy-white spot at base of bill, most conspicuous in breeding season. White secondaries visible in flight.

Call: Noisy: shrill, whinnying trill and loud, sharp 'chik' alarm note.

Habitat: Throughout, but rare in desert areas; usually in well-vegetated, still or slow-flowing freshwater areas.

Habits: Often runs pattering across surface of water with wings flapping.

Nesting: Breeds year round, mainly in spring and summer. Builds a floating heap of water plants low in the water, in which two to five white or bluish eggs are laid. These eggs hatch after about three weeks.

Notes: Small chicks are sometimes carried on the adult's back.

Status: Common resident.

Food: Small aquatic animals (frogs, tadpoles, fish, etc.).

Similar species: Non-breeding Black-necked Grebe has white cheeks and throat; when breeding, lacks the creamy spot at the base of the bill.

Eastern White Pelican

Pelecanus onocrotalus

Other names: Witpelikaan (A); ingcwanguba (X); ivubu & ifuba (Z).

Average size: Length 140–180cm; wingspan 272–305cm (m), 226–266cm (f).

Identification: Very large, mostly white, tinged with pink when breeding. Pink bill with yellowish pouch; pink legs. Wings black-and-white in flight. Immature[G] is browner, but lightens in colour with age.

Call: Usually silent; may grunt or moo in breeding colonies.

Habitat: Low-lying areas of the west and east, on open water bodies, coastal bays and estuaries.

Habits: Usually gregarious[G]. Forages in coordinated groups, forming a 'net' around fish.

Nesting: Year round. Nests in colonies of thousands. Up to three eggs are laid and hatch after six weeks. Both sexes incubate[G] and feed young.

Notes: Can swallow fish weighing up to 4kg.

Status: Locally common resident.

Food: Fish, but they also scavenge.

Similar species: Pink-backed Pelican is smaller and greyer.

Cape Gannet

Morus capensis

Other names:
Witmalgas (A);
umkholonjane (X).

Average size: Length 84–94cm;
wingspan 171–185cm;
wing 45–51cm.

Identification: Body mainly white,
with straw-yellow head. Cobalt
blue ring around the eye; heavy,
long, pointed, pale blue-grey bill;
long black line down centre of
throat; black, pointed tail.

Call: Raucous, rasping calls
when feeding and at
breeding colonies.

Habitat: Along
entire coast; offshore
coastal waters.

Habits: These
gregarious^G, aggressive
birds may plunge-dive
for fish from considerable
heights. They are
known for their 'sky-
pointing' displays^G.

Nesting: Mainly in
summer. Monogamous^G.

Nest is a guano^G platform with
a hollow top, in which one
egg is laid. Incubation^G, by both
sexes, is done with webs of feet.
The egg hatches after about
six weeks.

Notes: Hundreds of these
birds follow the 'sardine run'
up the KwaZulu-Natal coast
each winter.

Status: Common resident;
breeding endemic^G.

Food: Fish.

Similar species: None.

Cape Cormorant

Phalacrocorax capensis

Other names: Trekduiker (A); ugwidi (X).

Average size: Length 61–65cm; wingspan 109cm.

Identification: Mainly glossy blue-black; yellow throat; turquoise eye.

Call: Usually silent; clucks and croaks at breeding colonies.

Habitat: Coastal waters along the entire coast.

Habits: Highly gregarious[G]; it flies in long lines over the sea before settling in large flocks to feed by diving from the surface. Aggressive when breeding.

Nesting: Breeds in dense colonies year round, but mainly in spring. Nest is a shallow bowl of sticks, in which up to five pale, blue-green eggs are laid, which hatch after about three weeks. Both sexes incubate[G].

Notes: These birds provide a valuable annual harvest of guano[G], particularly off the coast of Namibia.

Status: Resident; breeding endemic[G].

Food: Fish, crustaceans.

Similar species: Bank Cormorant lacks yellow facial skin. Crowned Cormorant has a forecrown crest.

African Darter

Anhinga rufa

Other names: Afrikaanse Slanghalsvoël (A); ivuzi (X).

Average size: Length 80cm; wing 33–36cm.

Identification: Dark above, rufous[G] below, with white streaks on wings. Long, kinked neck; long tail and straight, pointed bill.

Call: Usually silent; croaks harshly on nest.

Habitat: Widespread on inland waters, estuaries and lagoons.

Habits: Swims low in the water. Dives well and spears fish underwater with bill. Roosts[G] communally.

Nesting: Year round. Builds platform of sticks and reeds in which two to seven greenish or bluish eggs are laid. These hatch after three to four weeks. Both parents incubate[G] and feed young.

Notes: Darters are sometimes

called 'Snakebirds' because of their habit of swimming with their entire body submerged, with only the head and neck showing above the water. Often seen sitting with their wings outspread, a habit they share with cormorants.

Status: Common resident.

Food: Fish, frogs, arthropods.

Similar species: Cormorants lack the rufous[G]-coloured, kinked neck, and have hooked bills.

Little Egret

Egretta garzetta

Other names: Kleinwitreier (A); ingekle (Z).

Average size: Length 65cm; wing 24–30cm.

Identification: All-white plumage. Black bill and legs; yellow feet.

Call: Gargling, chattering and harsh, heron-like croak at take-off.

Habitat: Virtually throughout the region; always near water.

Habits: Usually solitary^G when feeding, but roosts^G in groups. When feeding, may disturb bottom-dwelling prey by shuffling foot in pool bottom.

Nesting: Mainly in summer. Nests colonially^G, building platform of sticks on which two to four pale greenish-blue eggs are laid. These hatch after about three weeks. Both sexes incubate^G and feed young.

Notes: This bird was once hunted extensively for its plumes, called 'aigrettes', which were used to adorn dresses and hats.

Status: Common resident.

Food: Fish, frogs, insects.

Similar species: Great White Egret is larger and has black feet; Yellow-billed Egret has yellow bill; Cattle Egret has short yellow bill.

Hamerkop

Scopus umbretta

Other names: Hamerkop (A); uthekwane & uqhimng-qoshe (X); uthekwane (Z).

Average size: Length 56cm; wingspan 90–94cm.

Identification: Plain dark brown. Large bill and heavy crest giving 'hammerhead' appearance.

Call: Noisy yelping and squawking.

Habitat: Virtually throughout; most common in east. Occurs on inland waters (dams, lakes, rivers).

Habits: Usually solitary[G] or in small groups. Wades about in shallow water in search of food, occasionally stirring pool bottom with foot.

Nesting: Year round, mainly in spring. Builds huge, oven-shaped nest of sticks, reeds and debris (sometimes cooperatively with up to four other birds) with a small side entrance. Lays up to five white eggs, which hatch after about a month. Both sexes incubate[G].

Notes: The nest can take up to six months to build and measure up to 2m in diameter; it is so strong that a man can stand on its roof. It is often taken over by other birds or bees.

Status: Common resident.

Food: Frogs, fish.

Similar species: None.

African Sacred Ibis

Threskiornis aethiopicus

Other names: Skoorsteenveër (A); umxwagele (Z).

Average size: Length 90cm; wing 38cm.

Identification: Large. Mostly white plumage. Naked black head and neck; long, black bill curves downward. In flight, wings are white with black tips and trailing edges.

Call: Usually silent; croaks and squeals in breeding colonies.

Habitat: Varied: inland waters, cultivated lands, sewage works and rubbish dumps, and coastal lagoons. Mainly in southern and eastern regions.

Habits: Gregarious[G], with flocks sometimes numbering in hundreds. Feeds on ground; scavenges in farming areas. Roosts[G] in trees, reedbeds or on islands.

Nesting: Spring and summer. In courtship, may inflate neck like a balloon. Nests colonially[G], building stick platforms. Lays two to five eggs, which hatch after about a month. Both sexes incubate[G] and feed young.

Notes: This bird was once revered in Ancient Egypt.

Status: Common resident.

Food: Varied: arthropods, small mammals, nestling birds, eggs, small reptiles, carrion, seeds.

Similar species: None.

Greater Flamingo

Phoenicopterus roseus

Other names: Grootflamink (A); ukholwase & unondwebu (Z).

Average size: Length 127–140cm; wing 40–46cm (m), 36–39cm (f).

Identification: Large, with a long neck and long legs. Generally pale pink to white.

Pink bill with black tip, bent in middle; pink legs. Bright-red forewing seen in flight.

Call: Goose-like honking.

Habitat: Patchily throughout, on freshwater lakes, salt pans, estuaries, coastal lagoons.

Habits: Highly gregarious[G], flocks often numbering in thousands. Feeds by wading with bill upsidedown in water, sifting through mud. Swims in deeper water.

Nesting: After summer rains. Nests in dense colonies. Mud nest is volcano-shaped. One pale blue egg is laid and is incubated[G] for about a month by both parents.

Status: Common but nomadic resident.

Food: Aquatic insects, crustaceans, molluscs, microscopic algae.

Similar species: Lesser Flamingo is smaller and redder overall, and has a dark red bill.

Blue Crane

Anthropoides paradiseus

Other names:
Bloukraanvoël (A);
indwe (X);
indwa (Z).

Average size: Length
100–107cm; wing 51–59cm.

Identification: Blue-grey, with
long, slate-grey feathers, curving
to the ground like tail streamers.
White crown.

Call: Noisy; high-pitched,
guttural, rattling 'kraaank'.

Habitat: Vlei edges, grassland
and agricultural lands in
southern and eastern South
Africa, and at Etosha Pan
in Namibia.

Habits: In pairs or family groups
when breeding, otherwise highly
gregarious[G]. Roosts[G] in flocks.

Nesting: Display[G] dances
performed in pairs or groups.
In summer, lays one to three
pinkish-brown eggs on bare
ground, sometimes surrounding
eggs with bits of grass or
pebbles. The eggs hatch after
about a month.

Notes: South Africa's
national bird.

Status: Fairly common
resident; endemic[G].

Food: Frogs, insects, reptiles,
fish, grain, grass.

Similar species: Grey-
coloured herons lack the
long tertial plumes.

Red-knobbed Coot

Fulica cristata

Other names: Bleshoender (A); unomkqayi & unompemvana (X).

Average size: Length 44cm; wingspan 75–85cm.

Identification: All black, with white bill and frontal shield backed by two dark red knobs, which swell and become more visible during breeding season.

Call: Resonant clucking; snorting alarm call.

Habitat: Virtually throughout, on inland waters, sometimes slow-flowing rivers, coastal lagoons.

Habits: Usually in pairs or large flocks; gregarious^G when not breeding. Swims about on open water; forages by diving and grazing along the shoreline. Can swim long distances.

Nesting: Breeds year round, making nest of large heap of water plants in open water. Lays three to nine eggs, which hatch after about three weeks. Both sexes care for chicks, sometimes dividing the brood between them.

Notes: Toes are lobed, not webbed as in ducks.

Status: Common to abundant resident.

Food: Water plants, seeds, aquatic insects.

Similar species: Common Moorhen has a red frontal shield and yellow bill tip.

Egyptian Goose

Alopochen aegyptiaca

Other names:
Kolgans (A);
ilowe (X);
ilongwe (Z).

Average size: Length 63–73cm;
wing 34–41cm.

Identification: Mainly buff-brown above. Dark brown eye mask; dark brown patch on centre of breast. Metallic-green secondaries. In flight, shows conspicuous white forewings.

Call: Hissing (male only) and honking; calls with neck outstretched.

Habitat: Throughout the region, except in deserts. Occurs on inland waters, estuaries and coastal lakes, and in cultivated fields.

Habits: Gregarious[G] when not breeding, otherwise in pairs. Wary, quickly flies off when approached.

Nesting: Monogamous[G]. Breeds year round, mainly in spring. Lays five to 11 cream-coloured eggs, which hatch after about a month. Female incubates[G]; both parents feed young.

Notes: It is valued as a gamebird. Can become an agricultural pest.

Status: Very common resident.

Food: Grass, leaves, seeds, grain, aquatic rhizomes and tubers.

Similar species: South African Shelduck lacks brown eye mask and breast patch.

African Fish Eagle

Haliaeetus vocifer

Other names: Visarend (A); unomakhwezana (X); inkwazi (Z).

Average size: Length 63–73cm; wingspan 191cm (m), 237cm (f).

Identification: Dark body and wings; white head, nape and breast. Short, square, white tail. Dark chestnut belly and forewings. Female is larger.

Call: Unmistakable, ringing 'kyow-kyow-kow'.

Habitat: Mainly in north, east and south on large water bodies, lagoons and estuaries.

Habits: Usually in pairs. Hunts from a perch, stooping[G] at fish and catching them in its claws. Steals food from other birds, raids waterbird colonies and scavenges.

Nesting: Mainly in winter. Builds large stick nest, in which up to three white eggs are laid. These hatch after about six weeks. Both sexes incubate[G]; nestlings fed mostly by female.

Notes: Very vocal; one of the best-known and most studied birds.

Status: Locally common resident.

Food: Fish, carrion, nestlings and eggs, small mammals, lizards, frogs, insects.

Similar species: Palmnut Vulture has extensive white in the wing and a bare facial patch around the eye.

Black-shouldered Kite

Elanus caeruleus

Other names: Blouvalk (A); umdlampuku & unongwevana (X).

Average size: Length 33cm; wingspan 74cm.

Identification: Pale grey above, white below. Diagnostic[G] black shoulder patches. Black bill with yellow cere; yellow feet; red eye.

Call: Wheezy 'peeu' whistles and screams; soft 'weeep-weeep'.

Habitat: Virtually throughout, in varied habitats (agricultural areas; also grassland, woodland, savanna, semiarid scrub).

Habits: Solitary[G] or in pairs by day; roosts[G] communally at night. Hunts from perch or by hovering over prey.

Nesting: Year round, mainly in rainy seasons; may breed several times a year. Both sexes build a small stick platform on which two to six eggs are laid. Incubation[G], mostly by female, takes a month.

Notes: Very common; often seen perched on telephone poles.

Status: Common resident.

Food: Mainly rodents; also small birds, reptiles and insects.

Similar species: Lizard Buzzard has black streak down throat and two broad, white tail bands.

White-backed Vulture

Gyps africanus

Other names: Afrikaanse Witrug-aasvoël (A).

Average size: Length 90–98cm; wingspan 212–228cm.

Identification: Large. Generally streaky brown. Blackish face and neck. White lower back in flight. Dark eyes.

Call: Goose-like hisses, cackles and squeals; grunts.

Habitat: Northern half of region, in savanna and bushveld.

Habits: Gregarious[G]. Roosts[G] in trees at night; often rests on ground during day. Drinks and bathes regularly at waterholes.

Nesting: In winter. Builds platform of sticks high in a tree; may use nest for a few years. One white egg is laid. Both sexes incubate[G]; egg hatches after about two months. Both sexes feed young.

Notes: The most common vulture in southern Africa, and the most frequently seen in bushveld game reserves.

Status: Locally common.

Food: Carrion (softer parts of large game mammals), bone fragments.

Similar species: Cape Vulture is larger and paler, has yellow eyes and lacks white back.

Ostrich

Struthio camelus

Other names: Volstruis (A); inciniba (X); intshe (Z).

Height: Male up to 2m tall.

Identification: Very large. Long, grey, bristly neck; long legs. Male mostly black, with mostly white wings and white, buff or rufous[G] tail. Female brownish-grey.

Call: Deep, booming, lion-like roar, made at night.

Habitat: Virtually throughout, in bushveld to desert.

Habits: Sociable; often seen in groups of up to 10 birds. Forages among short vegetation.

Nesting: Year round. Males perform elaborate courtship displays[G] in breeding season. Nest is scrape in sandy soil in which up to 43 eggs are laid by several females. These hatch after six to seven weeks.

Notes: Flightless; the largest bird in the world. Can run at speeds of up to 60km/h. The only wild ostriches are in Namibia and the Kalahari. Ostriches are farmed for their feathers, skin, eggs and flesh.

Status: Resident.

Food: Mainly herbivorous (grass, berries, seeds, succulent plants); sometimes small reptiles, insects.

Similar species: None.

Common Moorhen

Gallinula chloropus

Other names: Grootwaterhoender (A).

Average size: Length 30–36cm; wingspan 45cm.

Identification: Dull, sooty black except for white undertail and white streaks on flanks. Red eye; red bill with yellow tip; red frontal shield.

Call: Sharp, nasal 'kirrik' or 'kik-kik-kik'; murmuring 'mook'.

Habitat: Practically throughout, on virtually any freshwater body surrounded by reeds and tall grasses.

Habits: Solitary^G or in small family groups. Flicks tail when alarmed. Flies heavily, with legs dangling.

Nesting: Year round; may raise up to eight broods a year. Territorial^G when breeding. Both sexes build bowl of rushes and reeds above water level. Lays four to nine eggs, which hatch after about three weeks. Female incubates^G during the day, male by day and night.

Notes: One of the most widely distributed birds in the world.

Status: Common resident.

Food: Mainly vegetable matter (water plants, seeds, berries); also molluscs, worms, spiders, insects, tadpoles.

Similar species: Lesser Moorhen is smaller and bill is mainly yellow; Lesser Gallinule has more colourful plumage and lacks white on flanks.

Helmeted Guineafowl

Numida meleagris

Other names: Gewone Tarentaal (A); impangele (X); impangele (Z).

Average size: Length 53–58cm; wing 24–29cm.

Identification: Slate-grey body, finely spotted with white. Small, naked, blue-and-red head. Prominent 'helmet'.

Call: Grating 'cherrrrr' or staccato 'kek-kek-kek' alarm call; also whistles.

Habitat: Virtually throughout, in grassland, vleis, savanna, cultivated lands, bushveld.

Habits: Gregarious^G; flocks may number in hundreds. Roosts^G communally in trees at night.

Nesting: Mainly in summer, in long grass or under bush. Six to 19 light yellowish-brown eggs are laid. They hatch after about a month. Only female incubates^G.

Notes: More than one female may lay eggs in the same nest,

producing a combined clutch of up to 50 eggs.

Status: Common resident.

Food: Seeds, bulbs, tubers, berries, insects, snails, ticks.

Similar species: Crested Guineafowl has black head plumes.

Blacksmith Lapwing (Plover)

Vanellus armatus

Other names: Bontkiewiet (A); indudumela (Z).

Average size: Length 30cm; wing 20–22cm.

Identification: Bold black, white and grey coloration. Grey wings; black nape, face, back and breast; white forehead, crown and belly. Ruby-red eye.

Call: Piercing 'klink-klink-klink'.

Habitat: Throughout, on shorelines of dams and sewage ponds, playing fields, tidal flats in bays and lagoons.

Habits: Solitary[G] or in pairs; non-breeders gather in flocks. Wary by nature, but aggressive in defence of their nest.

Nesting: Year round. Nest is a scrape on open ground, often near water. Two to four well-patterned eggs are laid; these hatch after about a month. Both sexes incubate[G].

Notes: Its call, which sounds like a hammer on an anvil, gave rise to its common name.

Status: Common resident.

Food: Insects, spiders, worms, small molluscs.

Similar species: Long-toed Lapwing has white face and foreneck.

Crowned Lapwing (Plover)

Vanellus coronatus

Other names:
Kroonkiewiet (A);
igxiya (X).

Average size: Length 30cm;
wing 19–22cm.

Identification: Mainly
greyish-brown; dark band
separating brown breast from
white belly. Black crown,
ringed with white 'halo'.
Long red legs.

Call: Very noisy: strident
'kreeep'.

Habitat: Virtually throughout,
in short grasslands and other
lawn-like habitats.

Habits: Gregarious[G] when
not breeding. Often active
at night.

Nesting: Mostly in spring. Two
to four well-marked, dark olive-
brown eggs are laid in shallow
scrape in ground. Both sexes
incubate[G]; eggs hatch after
about a month.

Notes: Quick to react to
disturbance, will scream at
intruders; birds
with young or
hatching eggs will
noisily 'divebomb'
intruders.

Status: Common
resident.

Food:
Arthropods.

Similar species:
No other similarly
sized lapwing has
a white halo and a
black crown.

Kelp Gull

Larus dominicanus

Other names: Swartrugmeeu (A); ingaba-ngaba (X).

Average size: Length 50–60cm; wingspan 127–132cm.

Identification: Large. Mostly white, with black back and wings. Heavy yellow bill with red spot near tip; olive legs.

Call: Loud 'kee-ow'; mewing; screams in defence at nest.

Habitat: Along entire coast; most abundant on west coast. Common in estuaries, beaches, harbours and rubbish dumps.

Habits: Forages by walking or flying. Follows ships for scraps and scavenges at harbours. Pilfers nests of other seabirds, taking eggs and small young. Steals food from other seabirds.

Nesting: Mainly in summer. Nest is a scrape on the ground, in which up to three pale green-, blue- or olive-splotched eggs are laid. These hatch after about a month. Both sexes incubate[G].

Status: Common to abundant resident.

Food: Fish, offal, invertebrates, birds' eggs and young birds.

Similar species: Lesser Black-backed Gull is smaller and has yellow legs.

Speckled Pigeon

Columba guinea

Other names: Kransduif (A); ivukuthu (X); ijub & ivukuthu (Z).

Average size: Length 33cm; wing 22–24cm.

Identification: Large pigeon with mostly grey head and underparts; bare red patch around eye. Reddish-brown wings are conspicuously spotted with white.

Call: Deep 'hooo-hooo-hooo' and mellow cooing.

Habitat: Virtually throughout, on mountains, cliffs and in urban areas.

Habits: Solitary^G or gregarious^G. Feeds by day in agricultural lands.

Nesting: Year round. Nest is platform of sticks and grass built on a ledge, rarely in trees. The two white eggs hatch after about two weeks. Both parents incubate^G and feed young.

Notes: Sometimes hybridises^G with Feral Pigeons.

Status: Common resident.

Food: Seeds, fallen grain, green shoots.

Similar species: Feral Pigeon lacks white-spotted wings; Rameron Pigeon is larger, darker and has yellow legs, eye patch and bill.

Laughing Dove

Streptopelia senegalensis

Other names: Rooiborsduifie (A); uvelemaxhoseni (X); ukhonzane (Z).

Average size: Length 26cm; wing 13–15cm.

Identification: Small; deep rufous^G chest spotted with red. Pinkish-grey head. Cinnamon back.

Call: Bubbling cooing, rising then falling.

Habitat: A wide range of habitats, but avoids forests.

Habits: Like other doves, depends on surface water and drinks daily.

Nesting: Year round, mainly in dry season. Up to four white eggs are laid; these hatch after about two weeks. Both parents incubate^G and feed young; 'pigeon's milk'

(regurgitated from the crop) is fed to hatchlings.

Notes: Probably the best-known of all our doves, it is found all over and has adapted well to cities and gardens. Its common name derives from its laughing call.

Status: Abundant resident.

Food: Seeds, grain, termite alates, insects and larvae, snails.

Similar species: Cape Turtle Dove has black hind collar.

Grey Go-away-bird (Lourie)

Corythaixoides concolor

Other names:
Kwêvoël (A);
umklewu (Z).

Average size: Length 47–50cm;
wing 21–23cm.

Identification: Large. Plain ash-grey all over, with long, shaggy head crest and long tail. Black bill, legs and feet.

Call: Nasal 'g'way' or 'kweh-h-h'; also grunts and shrieks.

Habitat: In north of region, in bushveld, savanna, riverine woodland and arid country; also suburban gardens.

Habits: In pairs or small groups. Quick and agile, but with a laboured flight. Highly vocal, especially when disturbed. Raises and lowers crest when alarmed.

Nesting: Year round. Builds platform of sticks in a tree, on which it lays two or three pale bluish-white eggs. These take about four weeks to hatch. Both sexes incubate[G] and feed young by regurgitation.

Notes: This bird is sometimes known as the 'Go-away-bird' on account of its call.

Status: Common resident.

Food: Fruit, flowers, buds, leaves, seeds.

Similar species: None.

Spotted Eagle-Owl

Bubo africanus

Other names: Gevlekte Ooruil (A); ifubesi (X); isikhovampondo (Z).

Average size: Length 43–50cm; wing 32–37cm.

Identification: Large. Grey above, sparsely spotted with white; finely barred dark grey below. Brown spots on breast. Yellow eyes. Very noticeable 'ear tufts'.

Call: Soft, hooting 'hu-hoo'; hissing in defence.

Habitat: Throughout, in rocky areas, woodland, savanna and gardens.

Habits: Solitary[G] or in pairs. Nocturnal, roosting[G] by day and hunting by night.

Nesting: Mostly winter and spring. Usually lays two white eggs in a scrape. Eggs hatch after about a month. Female incubates[G].

Notes: Most common large owl in the region. Rare rufous[G] colour form occurs, closely resembling Cape Eagle-Owl.

Status: Common resident.

Food: Arthropods, birds, reptiles, small mammals, frogs.

Similar species: Cape Eagle-Owl is heavily blotched, not barred, below, and has orange eyes.

Barn Owl

Tyto alba

Other names:
Nonnetjie-
uil (A);
isikhova (X);
isikhova (Z).

Average size: Length 30–34cm;
wing 24–30cm.

Identification: Pale tawny and
grey above, with small white
spots; whitish underparts, with
fine brown spots from breast to
belly. White, heart-shaped face
with small, dark eyes.

Call: Eerie, screeching 'schree';
hissing in defence.

Habitat: Throughout,
in woodland to desert;
avoids forest.

Habits: Usually in
pairs. Roosts[G] by day in
suitable cavity, often in
buildings. Weaves head
from side to side in
threat display[G].

Nesting: Throughout
year (varies regionally).
Two to 13 white eggs
are laid, over intervals of
up to three days, on flat floor
of suitable cavity. They hatch
after about a month. Female
incubates[G]. Nest may contain
range of growing young.

Notes: Found almost worldwide,
often in buildings, which gives
rise to its common name.

Status: Common resident.

Food: Rodents, small birds and
mammals, lizards, frogs, insects.

Similar species:
African Grass Owl is dark
brown above.

Pied Kingfisher

Ceryle rudis

Other names: Bontvisvanger (A); isaxwila (X); isiquba (Z).

Average size: Length 25–29cm; wing 13–15cm.

Identification: Distinctive black-and-white coloration. Black bill, legs and feet. Male has double breast band; female has single, incomplete breast band.

Call: High-pitched, rattling twitters and squeaks.

Habitat: Virtually throughout, on open water (rivers, lakes, dams, estuaries, coastal waters).

Habits: Usually in pairs or family groups. Hunts from perch or by hovering over water; beats prey against perch before swallowing.

Nesting: In spring and summer. Nests in burrow in sandbank, sometimes in small colonies. Lays two to six eggs. Incubation[G] period probably about two weeks.

Notes: Sometimes breeds cooperatively, with young of previous brood helping to rear the new chicks.

Status: Common resident.

Food: Mostly fish, some crustaceans and insects.

Similar species: Giant Kingfisher is much larger with rufous[G] breast.

African Hoopoe

Upupa africana

Other names: Afrikaanse Hoephoep (A); ubhobhoyi (X); uziningweni (Z).

Average size: Length 25–28cm; wing 13–15cm.

Identification: Dove-sized. Orange-brown head, back and underparts; black-tipped crest; boldly black-and-white-barred wings; black tail with white base. Long, thin bill curves slightly downward. Short legs.

Call: 'Hoop-hoop-hoop'.

Habitat: Throughout, in woodland, gardens, parks, thornveld.

Habits: Usually solitary[G] or in pairs. Probes ground with bill, looking for food. Raises crest on alighting or when alarmed.

Nesting: Spring and summer. Nests in existing hole; rears up to three broods per season. Lays up to six eggs, which hatch after about three weeks. Female incubates[G].

Notes: Its nest becomes very dirty and smelly, probably deterring predators.

Status: Common resident.

Food: Insects, earthworms, small snakes, frogs, termites, lizards.

Similar species: None.

Crested Barbet

Trachyphonus vaillantii

Other names: Kuifkophout-kapper (A).

Average size: Length 23cm; wing 9–11cm.

Identification: Yellow face and underparts, streaked red; small black crest and black breast band. Upperparts blackish, scalloped white; rump red.

Call: Penetrating trilling by male; answering 'puka-puka' by female.

Habitat: In northern and eastern regions in woodland, forest, dry savanna, parks, gardens.

Habits: Common in suburban gardens.

Nesting: Breeds throughout year, mainly in spring and summer; may rear up to four broods per season. Both sexes dig nest holes, in which two to four white eggs are laid. These hatch after about two weeks. Both male and female incubate[G] eggs and feed chicks.

Notes: Territorial[G]; does not tolerate other bird species.

Food: Mainly insects; also fruit, snails and birds' eggs.

Similar species: Yellow-headed form of Black-collared Barbet has a black bill, olive back, rump and wings, and lacks crest.

Fork-tailed Drongo

Dicrurus adsimilis

Other names: Mikstert-byvanger (A); intengu (X); intengu (Z).

Average size: Length 23–25cm; wing 13–14cm.

Identification: Longish, deeply notched tail. Red eyes.

Call: Loud, jumbly, discordant song; also imitates other birds, including Pearlspotted Owl.

Habitat: Avoids forest interiors and open habitats.

Habits: Bold and aggressive. Flies out from perch to catch prey; returns to perch to eat its catch.

Nesting: Mainly in summer; may raise two or three broods per season. Lays two to four eggs, which hatch after about three weeks.

Notes: Occasionally plunge-dives to catch fish.

Status: Common resident.

Food: Insects (bees), small birds, fish, lizards.

Similar species: Square-tailed Drongo and Southern Black Flycatcher are smaller, and their tails are only slightly notched; latter has black eyes.

Pied Crow

Corvus albus

Other names: Witborskraai (A); igwangwa (X); igwababa (Z).

Average size: Length 46–52cm; wing 33–39cm.

Identification: Shiny black, with white breast and broad white collar around neck.

Call: Harsh, deep, loud 'kraaa'.

Habitat: Virtually throughout.

Habits: Scavenger. Frequents rubbish dumps; forages on ground. Also catches small birds in flight.

Nesting: Mainly in spring and summer. Builds large nest in tall tree or on telephone pole. Lays up to seven eggs, which hatch after about three weeks.

Notes: Intelligent and cocky, struts about with arrogant confidence. Sometimes harasses large birds of prey at carcasses.

Status: Common resident.

Food: Seeds, fruit, frogs, reptiles, fish, birds, eggs, small mammals, ectoparasites (on game mammals), carrion (usually road kill).

Similar species: White-necked Raven lacks white breast and has shorter tail and larger head. House Crow is smaller, with grey breast and collar.

Dark-capped Bulbul

Pycnonotus tricolor

Other names: Swartoogtiptol (A); ikhwebula (X); iphothwe (Z).

Average size: Length 20–22cm; wing 10cm.

Identification: Smallish. Slightly crested, black head. Dark eye ring. Greyish-brown back; dark brown breast, whitish belly, lemon-yellow undertail.

Call: Lively, liquid notes.

Habitat: In north and east, in wide variety of habitats; woodland, forest edge, plantations, gardens.

Habits: Usually in pairs. Very vocal and conspicuous, often calls from top of trees.

Nesting: Year round, mainly in spring and summer. Cup of dry grass and twigs built in tree. Two or three eggs are laid, which hatch after about two weeks.

Female incubates[G]; male feeds her while she is on the nest.

Notes: Mobs and scolds owls, hawks and snakes. Sometimes known as 'Toppies'. Parasitised[G] by Jacobin Cuckoo.

Status: Abundant resident.

Food: Fruit, nectar, insects, lizards.

Similar species: Cape Bulbul has white eye wattle; African Red-eyed Bulbul has red eye wattle; Terrestrial Bulbul has white throat.

Olive Thrush

Turdus olivaceus

Other names: Olyflyster (A); umswi (X); umunswi (Z).

Average size: Length 24cm; wing 13cm.

Identification: Dark olive-brown above. Grizzled white throat. Dull orange underparts, washed olive at sides.

Call: Thin 'tseep' alarm and take-off call; fluty, trilling song.

Habitat: Montane forests, parks, gardens and plantations. Confined largely to South Africa.

Habits: Usually singly or in pairs. Forages energetically on ground, scratching in fallen leaves and debris. Begins singing every morning before dawn.

Nesting: Year round, mostly in spring and summer. Nest is large bowl built in tree. Up to four eggs are laid. These are incubated[G] by female and hatch after two weeks. Both sexes feed young.

Notes: Although shy in forest habitats, this bird is bolder in suburban gardens.

Status: Common resident.

Food: Insects, molluscs, spiders, small lizards, fruit, seeds.

Similar species: Kurrichane Thrush is smaller, and has an orange eye ring and black malar stripes. Orange Ground Thrush shows white bars on folded wings.

Cape Robin-Chat

Cossypha caffra

Other names: Gewone Janfrederik (A); ugaga (X); umbhekle (Z).

Average size: Length 16–18cm; wing 8–9cm.

Identification: Black face with white eyebrow. Light orange throat and breast. Grey belly. Orange tail with black centre.

Call: Melodious whistling; often sings before dawn.

Habitat: South Africa, southern Namibia and eastern Zimbabwe, in forest edge, montane scrub, fynbos, gardens, parks and farmlands.

Habits: Usually solitary[G] or in pairs. Keeps mostly to dense undergrowth; sings from perch.

Nesting: Regionally variable. Male builds nest on ground or in hole, in which up to four eggs are laid. These hatch after about two weeks. Female incubates[G]; both sexes feed young.

Notes: Parasitised[G] by Red-chested Cuckoo; as soon as cuckoo hatches, it evicts robin's own young from nest.

Status: Common resident.

Food: Insects, spiders, worms, small frogs, lizards, fruit.

Similar species: Chorister Robin-Chat and Heuglin's Robin-Chat are wholly orange below; White-throated Robin-Chat has white throat and breast.

Cape Wagtail

Motacilla capensis

Other names: Gewone Kwikkie (A); umcelu (X); umvemve (Z).

Average size: Length 18–20cm; wing 8cm.

Identification: Dull greyish-brown above; dull off-white below. Narrow, slate-grey breast-band. Creamy-white eyebrow.

Call: Clear, piping 'tseep'; whistled, trilling song.

Habitat: Near water, parks and gardens.

Habits: Usually solitary[G] or in pairs. Gregarious[G] when not breeding. Forages energetically on ground. Wags tail up and down.

Nesting: Year round, mainly in spring and summer; may raise up to four broods per season. Builds bulky nest, well concealed, in which up

to seven putty-coloured eggs are laid; these hatch after about two weeks. Both parents incubate[G] and feed young.

Notes: A rather dull bird compared with other wagtails of the region.

Status: Common resident.

Food: Insects, small fish, tadpoles, food scraps.

Similar species: African Pied Wagtail is strikingly black-and-white; Long-tailed Wagtail has longer tail, white underparts and clearer grey underparts.

Common Fiscal

Lanius collaris

Other names: Gewone Fiskaallaksman (A); inxanxadi (X); iqola (Z).

Average size: Length 21–23cm; wing 9–10cm.

Identification: Black above, white below; at rest shows bold white 'V' on back. Longish, white-edged black tail. Heavy, hooked bill.

Call: Piping and grating notes; also imitates other birds.

Habitat: Virtually throughout, except in forest and desert.

Habits: Territorial^G. Perches conspicuously. May be very aggressive towards other birds.

Nesting: Year round; may raise several broods per season. Female builds thick-walled bowl in tree, in which up to five eggs are laid; these hatch after about two weeks. Both sexes feed chicks.

Notes: Often seen in gardens, where it chases off other bird species. Known as 'Jackie Hangman' for its habit of impaling uneaten prey on thorns or spikes.

Status: Common resident.

Food: Insects, small lizards, frogs and birds.

Similar species: Fiscal Flycatcher has a slimmer bill and a shorter tail with conspicuous white side patches.

Fiscal Flycatcher

Sigelus silens

Other names: Fiskaalvlieëvanger (A); icola (X).

Average size: Length 17–20cm; wing 9–10cm.

Identification: Male black above, female dark brown above. White below. Bold white wing stripe. Black tail with large, rectangular white stripes. Slender bill.

Call: Weak, chattering song.

Habitat: In thornveld, bush and scrub, exotic plantations and suburban gardens.

Habits: Usually solitary or in pairs. Bold and conspicuous. Sometimes catches insects in flight.

Nesting: Spring and summer. Two to four finely speckled, pale greenish-blue eggs are laid; these hatch after about two weeks.

Notes: Less aggressive than the Common Fiscal.

Status: Common resident; endemic[G].

Food: Insects, fruit, aloe nectar.

Similar species: Common Fiscal has longer tail, and stout, hooked bill.

Red-winged Starling

Onychognathus morio

Other names:
Rooivlerkspreeu (A);
isomi (X);
insomi (Z).

Average size: Length 27–29cm;
wing 14–16cm.

Identification: Large, elegant
bird with dark eyes, short legs
and long tail. Male glossy blue-
black; female has a grey head.
Rich chestnut flight feathers.

Call: Melodius, whistling song.

Habitat: In mountainous areas
in south and east; also in
Okavango Delta.

Habits: Gregarious^G; in pairs
when breeding. Moves
with bounding hops. Bold
and conspicuous; highly
aggressive near nest,
'divebombing' intruders.

Nesting: In spring and summer.
Nest is bowl in which two to
four eggs are laid; these hatch
after two to three weeks.
Female incubates^G; both sexes
feed young.

Notes: One of the most familiar
starlings, readily adapted to city-
centre living; frequently nests on
buildings. Probes for ticks on the
backs of cows.

Status: Common
resident.

Food: Fruit,
insects, ticks,
millipedes,
lizards, aloe
nectar.

Similar species:
Pale-winged
Starling has pale
eyes and whitish
flight feathers.

Cape Glossy Starling

Lamprotornis nitens

Other names: Kleinglansspreeu (A); inyakrini (X); ikhwezi (Z).

Average size: Length 22–25cm; wing 12–15cm.

Identification: Iridescent blue-green, washed faintly greenish on ear coverts. Green belly and flanks. Bright orange-yellow eye.

Call: Distinctive, two-syllabled, 'turr-rree' callnote on take-off; pleasant, jumbled warblings.

Habitat: Virtually throughout; in savanna, bush, scrub, mixed woodland, urban areas.

Habits: In pairs when breeding, otherwise gregarious[G]; gathers in small flocks. Runs well.

Nesting: Mainly in spring and summer. Nest a pad in natural hole or under eaves in which two to four lightly speckled, light greenish-blue eggs are laid. Both sexes feed young, sometimes helped by young from previous broods.

Notes: Very similar to the blue-eared starlings.

Status: Common, widespread.

Food: Omnivorous.

Similar species: Greater Blue-eared Starling and Southern Lesser Blue-eared Starling have dark blue and magenta bellies respectively. Both have full ear patches.

Amethyst Sunbird

Chalcomitra amethystina

Other names:
Afrikaanse Swart-suikerbekkie (A); ingcungcu (X).

Average size: Length 15cm; wing 6–8cm.

Identification: Male mostly sootyblack, with bright metallic-green forehead and metallic-purple throat and rump. Female grey above, tinged olive, and creamy-white below; streaked blackish on throat and breast. Long, black bill curves downwards.

Call: Fast twittering and chattering.

Habitat: Forest edge, woodland, savanna, parks and gardens.

Habits: Usually solitary[G] or in pairs. Restless and aggressive. Often hovers when feeding.

Nesting: Varies regionally. Nest with side-top entrance, built by female, suspended from branch or built on wires or light fittings around houses. Up to three eggs are laid, which hatch after about two weeks. Female incubates[G] and feeds young.

Notes: Occasionally parasitised[G] by Klaas's Cuckoo.

Status: Common resident.

Food: Nectar, insects and spiders.

Similar species: Scarlet-chested Sunbird has large, scarlet breast patch. Dusky Sunbird is smaller and has a white belly.

House Sparrow

Passer domesticus

Other names: Huismossie (A).

Average size: Length 14cm; wing 7cm.

Identification: Brown above, with grey rump. Male has grey cap, reddish-brown back, white cheeks and black throat. Female is duller grey-brown and has off-white eye stripe.

Call: Sharp, harsh, penetrating chirps and cheeps.

Habitat: Throughout, always around human habitation.

Habits: In pairs or family groups when breeding, otherwise gregarious^G, sometimes in flocks of hundreds. Hops about on ground; sometimes hawks flying insects.

Nesting: Year round, mainly in spring and summer. Nest is untidy. Lays two to five eggs, which hatch after about two weeks. Both sexes incubate^G and feed young.

Notes: Most cosmopolitan bird in the world. Introduced in Durban in late 1800s and spread quickly, reaching northern areas of region by the 1960s.

Status: Common to abundant resident.

Food: Seeds, buds, fruit, insects, spiders, household scraps.

Similar species: Male Cape Sparrow has black face and cap; Great Sparrow is more rufous^G above and has chestnut rump.

Southern Red Bishop

Euplectes orix

Other names: Suidelike Rooivink (A); umlilo (X); ibomvana (Z).

Average size: Length 13cm; wing 6–8cm.

Identification: Breeding male has black breast, forehead, face and throat; rest of head, upperparts and breast-band brilliant orange-scarlet; brown wings and tail. Female and non-breeding male are boldly streaked buff and dark brown above; buffy eyebrow; dark brown wings and tail.

Call: Sharp 'chiz-chiz' call notes; wheezy, whiny song.

Habitat: Virtually throughout, except in arid and mountainous regions; on wetland fringes, gardens, fields and open grassland.

Habits: Gregarious[G]; forms dense colonies in reedbeds.

Nesting: In spring and summer, polygamous[G] male puffs out breast and displays[G] with bee-like flight. Male weaves nest, female lines it. Lays two to five eggs, which hatch in less than two weeks.

Notes: Nests often parasitised[G] by Diederick Cuckoo.

Status: Common, widespread resident.

Food: Seeds, insects.

Similar species: Fire-crowned Bishop breeding male has scarlet forecrown and black wings and tail.

Southern Masked Weaver

Ploceus velatus

Other names: Swartkeel-geelvink (A); ihobohobo (X); ihlokohloko (Z).

Average size: Length 14–16cm; wing 7–9cm.

Identification: Breeding male has black mask ending in point on upper breast; yellow hind crown and nape; red eye. Female lacks mask and is light olive-brownish above; whitish belly; brown eye.

Call: Harsh swizzling; sharp 'chik' alarm note.

Habitat: Virtually throughout; favours open habitats.

Habits: Gregarious^G, often breeding in large colonies. Displays^G by hanging under nest, fanning wings and swizzling.

Nesting: In winter, spring and summer; polygamous^G male may have up to eight broods a season. Nest is neat. Female lays two to four eggs, which are incubated^G by her and hatch

after about two weeks. Female feeds young.

Notes: The casanovas of the bird world: males have up to 12 nests.

Status: Common resident.

Food: Insects, seeds, flower parts, nectar.

Similar species: Spotted-backed Weaver has heavily spotted back; Lesser Masked Weaver has white eyes and grey legs.

Cape White-eye

Zosterops capensis

Other names: Kaapse Glasogie (A); intukwane (X); umehlwane (Z).

Average size: Length 12cm; wing 7cm.

Identification: Greyish-green above. Yellow throat and undertail. White eye-ring. Short bill. Some regional variation in colour.

Call: Long, jerky, reedy song; sweet, piping, trilled call notes.

Habitat: Throughout South Africa and in most parts of Namibia, in forest, woodland, savanna, parks and gardens, riverine scrub and bush.

Habits: In pairs when breeding; otherwise gregarious^G. Drinks and bathes frequently. Forages restlessly in undergrowth.

Nesting: In spring and summer, sometimes winter. Nest is a small, neat, thin-walled cup, in which two to four eggs are laid. Both sexes incubate^G eggs, which hatch in less than two weeks. Both sexes feed young.

Notes: One of the best-known garden birds of the region. Although considered a pest by some fruit-growers, they do also eat aphids and insects that are harmful to fruit.

Status: Common resident; endemic^G.

Food: Insects, spiders, nectar and fruit.

Similar species: Yellow White-eye is yellower above and has uniform, bright yellow underparts.

Cape Canary

Serinus canicollis

Other names: Kaapse Kanarie (A); umlonji (X); umzwilili (Z).

Average size: Length 13cm; wing 7cm.

Identification: Slender. Greenish-gold crown and face; rest of head blue-grey. Light olive, finely streaked back; dull yellow rump and yellow below. Longish, notched, olive tail with yellow margins.

Call: Very sweet, loud, clear trills and twitters.

Habitat: In south and east; favours mountainous habitats; also fynbos, grassland, gardens and parks.

Habits: Gregarious[G]. In pairs or small family groups when breeding; otherwise in flocks, sometimes numbering hundreds.

Nesting: Mainly in spring and summer, depending on locality. Female builds thick-walled cup in tree, in which two to five variably coloured eggs are laid; these hatch after about two weeks. Female incubates[G]; both sexes feed young.

Status: Common resident.

Food: Seeds, fruit, flowers.

Similar species: Yellow-eyed Canary has bolder, diagnostic[G] facial markings; Forest Canary is heavily streaked below and is darker above.

Glossary

Colonial: Associating in close proximity when nesting.

Diagnostic: Conclusively identifying a given bird (a bird that has a 'diagnostic' feature can be identified by that feature).

Display: Ritualised behaviour of a bird that wishes to attract a mate or defend a territory.

Endemic: A species whose breeding and non-breeding ranges are confined to one region (a species that breeds only in one region but moves away at other times is called a 'breeding endemic').

Gregarious: Living together in flocks.

Guano: The excrement of fish-eating seabirds, highly valued as fertilizer.

Host: A bird that incubates and rears another species' young (see 'Parasite').

Hybridise: Interbreed.

Immature: Not yet adult.

Incubate: To regulate egg temperature with the body.

Monogamous: Having only one mate during a breeding season.

Parasite (brood parasite): A bird ... eggs in other birds' nests (see 'Host'). Chicks are reared by the host.

Polygamous: Having more than one mate during a breeding season.

Roost: The place where birds rest or sleep.

Rufous: Reddish brown.

Solitary: Not living in organised colonies or large groups ('in pairs' means two birds are found together).

Stoop: Swoop down.

Territory: An area that a bird establishes and then defends against others; birds that defend a territory are called 'territorial'.